HOW TO AVOID BUSINESS FAILURE

Colin Myles

1

How to Avoid Business Failure

Copyright 2014
By Colin Myles

Formatting by www.busylizzie.ie

Table of Contents

Foreword

First off, every single entrepreneur in every village, town, city and country around the world deserves credit and a round of applause for crossing the line and starting their own business.

As time passes, it's sad to say, a lot of these ventures become a statistic. You know, the horrible one which states "90% of start-ups are gone within 2-5 years".

This book is aimed at the entrepreneur, small business and self-employed. The book will share with you 7 Steps to avoid business failure.

The purpose of this book is for you to identify, avoid and overcome these steps. To enable your business stay successful.'

The 7 Steps in this book are universal. Because you can learn and overcome these steps, no matter where in the world your business trades.

Because you have crossed the line and stepped out in faith, I simply want to share with you some things which, when prevented, could stop you becoming one of those horrible statistics.

> *"Anytime you see someone more successful than you are, they are doing something you aren't".*
>
> *- Malcolm X*

Colin Myles, February 2014
www.colinmyles.net

Chapter 1
No System

> *"Business is like a wheelbarrow – it stands still until someone pushes it".*
>
> *– Unknown*

No system is the first step in avoiding business failure. When all you seem to be doing is flying by the seat of your pants and firefighting each and every day.

Have you ever wondered how a McDonalds can operate with a group of kids seeming to run the show? Simple. They have a system, an operating manual anyone can follow. Do you have a system in place that enables your team to run the business when you are not there?

When you first start out, you are flying by the seat of your pants to some degree. Where does this go? How do we do that? What day do we re-order for re-stocking? How do we answer the phone, process orders and all the many seemingly mundane tasks that contribute to the success or failure of your business?

Imagine yourself going into a computer repair shop. The folks are really nice but you smell the air of confusion. They believe Tommy is the man to speak to, or is it Marcie? They have trouble finding the correct form to fill out. They stare at their screen, punch keys and mutter to themselves. Meanwhile you are standing there thinking "should I stay, go, or even trust them at all?"

Real nice folks but the message they are sending out is confusion. Is it their fault? Not really, not if there is no defined system to follow. Without a system they operate under the mantra "not sure, but it worked the last time". Quick question. Does your business operate like this? Hopefully your team operates with calm confidence at all times.

It does not matter the size of your business, you must have systems in place. Who is responsible for each area of your business? Who collects the money due? What is the acceptable level of your aged debtors lists? What is your social media strategy? How do you track sales and all the other items which I hope are not still on your to-do list.

One of the biggest moans people have when dealing with a business is that nobody can give them an answer. All that happens is they get passed from Billy to Bob and Mary to Marcie without anyone being able to give them a straight answer.

Your team, remember them. They like to know what they are doing. Most people dislike uncertainty. Your team, when uncertain how to handle questions, become nervous, flustered, appear incompetent and feel stupid because they have no system to follow.

Now the last thing you want is for your business to be portrayed as one where uncertainty rules. You have taken a brave step, your family wants your business to succeed and prosper.

So, stand back, take a hard look with stone cold eyes at your business. Are the systems there? If so, are they good enough to take you from where you are to where you want to be?

Take the time, sit down and write out all the systems you are carrying in your head, but have not yet conveyed to your team. You need to do this for your own well-being as well as for the health and success of your team and business.

Most importantly your customer, the person who pays the wages, needs to believe in you, your business, and its ability to solve their problems. A wise man once told me "no customers = no business"!

For you the equation goes something like this:

No systems = lost customers
Lost customers = no customers
No customers = no business

Hint: Putting systems in place allows you to work **on** your business not **in** the business

Chapter 2
Rude, Uninterested, Bored Staff

> *"One customer, well taken care of, could be more valuable than $10,000 worth of advertising".*
>
> *- Jim Rohn*

Another step to avoid is hiring and employing rude, uninterested and bored staff. Yes, when you walk into the room they may be attentive, busy little bees, but as soon as your back is turned their real selves come out to play.

R.U.B.S. will propel your business downwards quicker than you can spot them. You may see them elsewhere but sadly have a blind spot when it comes to your own. A quick way to gauge whether you have been infected by R.U.B.S. is to look at your customer churn. Do you engage in a constant battle to retain existing and gain new customers?

A number of years ago a survey came out which showed that 62% of your customers walked away, never to come back again, because of a sleight against them, real or imagined.

Picture yourself as a customer being shouted at, ignored or spoken to like you're an idiot, all because you asked a simple question.

Sad thing is it happens all the time across the globe. If it is happening in your business and you don't check it in time, your customers will leave and never tell you why. But they will tell everybody and anybody why they won't do business with you again.

A long time ago I came across the phrase "Everybody is somebody's somebody". That person a member of staff was rude to on the phone or in person could have been the favourite niece or nephew of your biggest customer. Can you imagine what they are going to tell them the next time they meet?

Envisage the wife of a client you have been trying to engage for the past six months, being rudely interrupted when making an enquiry. Can you hear what she is going to tell her husband over dinner that evening? Or the person who has saved for six months to buy a particular item from your store.

They walk in feeling proud and happy only to be greeted by people who have no interest in serving them. Most likely they will turn on their heels and make their purchase online from the comfort of their favourite chair.

There is an old adage in sales that it takes six months to gain a new customer and six seconds to lose them. Let's revisit the quote at the start of this chapter. A customer, well taken care of, could save you $10,000 in advertising. Have you got a spare ten grand to attract one new customer?

Six seconds of someone being rude, bored or uninterested is going to cost you $10,000. Write it down, imprint it on your brain. How long could your business survive with the rude, bored and uninterested leading the way?

Maybe the people you hired weren't that way in the beginning. Please put a system in place that catches this behaviour, nips it in the bud and stops this unhealthy virus killing your business. Killing your ability to look after and leave a legacy for your family.

You could spends thousands upon thousands sending people on customer care, customer excellence courses. They may have collected enough certificates to paper your living room. Still you must be eternally vigilant against the rude, bored and uninterested.

Become a six second vigilante. Six seconds = one lost customer = $10,000 to replace. You may have written down in detail who your ideal customer is. This is good but you must also write down, in detail, who your ideal employee is.

Time to step back, look at your team and how they interact with your current and future customers. Be ever vigilant for rude, uninterested and bored behaviour and attitudes.

Remember, 62% of your lost customers leave because of a slight against them, real or imagined. Six seconds to lose one customer, six months to gain a new one.

Can your business afford it?

Hint: Hire happy people.

Chapter 3
Bleed it Dry

> *"A good chief gives, he does not take".*
>
> *- Mohawk Proverb*

Now we come to one of those pesky and sneaky steps you must quickly learn to avoid. Because you do not want to be scrambling, splashing and struggling. Searching for a way to avoid your business being crushed.

Many times the temptation when business is booming, to take, take more and put nothing back in is the temptation that can't be resisted. The belief that this will last forever is a naive fallacy.

Your business needs to be nurtured. Flowers without water and nutrients, wither and die over time. A business that is not nurtured, wilts, stagnates and dies. The action of take, take without putting something back into the business that sustains your lifestyle, leads to the well running dry. The only thing left in your money chest will be angry letters from your bank and creditors.

Big, angry red letters on beautiful paper. Where once you were the master, now you become a slave. A slave to others. Is this what you want for you and your business?

Putting X amount of your profits back into your business to maintain, nurture and grow it is a must, not a sometimes thing, but an all the time action.

Imagine buying a brand new top-of-the-range automobile. It is beautiful, elegant, with sleek lines and up-to-date technology. To keep it moving and doing what it was made to do, you must fill it up with gasoline. People admire it, congratulate you on your purchase. You feel on top of the world. How long would it be able to do its job if you don't fill it up? Not long.

Automobiles can't run on fumes and neither can your business. You must re-invest to survive. So you now have a couple of choices, which path to follow. You can burn brightly like a shooting star for a short period, and disappear only to be a fleeting memory. Or you can look after, nurture and re-invest in your business to see it shine brightly forever and a day.

The temptation to take and not give is as old as time. The human mind, convinced the sea of green you have created will last forever without you nurturing it, is possibly the greatest trick your mind can play on you as a business owner.

Believing the money your business is pumping out entitles you to become king/queen of the long lunch brigade could not be further from the truth. It could be, but only if you make the decision to re-invest. Otherwise you will become one of those "used to be's|" and used to be don't pay no bills!

Take a look at your profits and decide right now you are going to re-invest X amount each month to nurture your business. X amount to feed it, X amount to maintain its smooth running, X amount to maintain your brand, X amount to maintain and stay ahead of the technology curve. Last but not least, X amount to maintain and enhance the fantastic customer experience your business is known for.

The list is endless. How soon will the sea of greenbacks run dry without you making sure the business is nurtured? How long will your business last with the attitude of take, take...? Truthful answer please. "You must give before you can receive". A very old but true saying.

My wish is for you to enjoy great rewards from your business. Rewards that will enable you to leave a legacy but also live a legacy. Don't be like a shooting star that shines brightly for a short period of time then disappears altogether.

As Les Brown says: "Used to be's don't pay no bills".

Chapter 4
Price Loyalty
(A race to the bottom)

> *"The bitterness of poor quality remains long after the sweetness of low price is forgotten".*
>
> *- Unknown*

Believing you can superglue customer loyalty to price means you have joined the race to the bottom. This race leads to one outcome, someone is going out of business. Your ability to stay away from this dangerous sport will determine how your business can avoid failure. It is a step known to overwhelm and debilitate even those with swift thought, clear minds and agile movement.

Most people enter business with the greatest of intentions - to give their customers a great product or service, combined with an outstanding customer experience. Somewhere along their journey they get distracted from the basic fundamentals and find themselves being pulled into the price race.

Believing you will attract loyal customers based on price is akin to believing in the tooth fairy. Nice bedtime story for the kids but no basis in reality.

The customer who comes to you because currently you have the lowest price, will leave you as quickly for the next person or company who beats that price. They have absolutely no interest in loyalty or rewarding outstanding customer experience.

As I write this, major retailers have been losing customers due to inventory challenges. Operators in the "pile 'em high, sell 'em cheap" brigade. Where have their loyal customers gone?

When you join the price race, lines start to become blurred and fuzzy. Quality product and outstanding service get lost in the flurry of price cuts. Slash, slash, cut, cut and in the end something has to go as you struggle to maintain your margins. What in essence goes is customer loyalty – the customers who appreciated quality and service.

You have joined the price tribe. Because of price cuts your margins are getting slimmer. To maintain your profits you need a greater volume of customers purchasing at a cheaper price. The price tribe migrates to cheaper prices.

When they do, your volume goes down along with your profits. If you agonise over them coming back, guess what, you have to cut prices again which means your profits are getting slimmer and you need a greater amount of the price tribe to cross your threshold to stay afloat.

A miracle. They come back and as soon as they do, your competitor cuts their price. The price tribe migrates back across the highway plains. How deep are your pockets? Welcome aboard the fantastic game, only one will win, ever decreasing circles.....

Ever decreasing circle of profits. In your desperation for people to buy from you, service gets kicked into touch. You promise yourself you will bring it back when things stabilise. You start ignoring quality to buy the cheapest product you can sell, at the cheapest price. All to keep the price tribes migrating in your direction. Will you keep your promise to bring back quality and service?

Let's go back to the quote at the start of this chapter and reflect. Along this helter-skelter journey of the price race, a subtle but surprising thing starts to happen. People start to notice the drop in quality of your product or service. The feeling of bitterness and resentment will overtake the sweet thrill of the low price.

When this happens, watch out. As your business generates bitterness and resentment, the price tribe will stop migrating in your direction. Your once loyal customers, who appreciated quality and service have long since moved on. Who is left?

It is a hard balancing act to keep price, quality and outstanding customer service all going at the same time. A three-legged stool only works when all three legs are firmly balanced on the floor, otherwise it is not fit for purpose.

When you start to favour the price leg of your business above quality and outstanding customer service, you create an imbalance and your business starts to wobble. How you react to this wobble and imbalance is entirely up to you, because it is your business and you have sole responsibility for its direction.

Hint: Should you decide to go down the route of competing on price, PLEASE TREAD CAREFULLY.

Chapter 5
No Innovation

"Innovation is the ability to see change as an opportunity, not a threat".

- Unknown

Your business must avoid the step, where you stop innovating. Because without innovation your chances of failure increase. You do not want your business to fail . . . do you?

I am a firm believer in the old saying "the only constant in life is change".

Hotels went from the old cord switchboard where you had to phone reception to get an outside line, to automatic switchboards. Now the majority of people use their own mobile phones or skype. People expect free Wi-Fi in their rooms. The changes being constant, constantly evolving innovation.

Innovation does not have to be a big shiny object that everyone comes to admire and kneel before. It comes in many forms that enable your business to perform better and provide an outstanding customer experience. Between those two pillars, big shiny and small incremental innovations that the ghost of failure looms.

Operating a billing and debt collecting system which leaves you with an aged debtors list of 60-90 days is a health warning to your business. Innovation has changed this and can help you run an aged debtors list of 30 days or less. Cash flow is king, use innovation to keep the cash moving.

What innovations do you use to save you time and increase the level of customer loyalty for your business? Are you taking advantage of social media, websites, blogs, newsletters, twitter, Facebook, google +, all of which were unheard of twenty years ago.

Your existing and potential customers are using and adapting to new innovations, making them part of the everyday fabric of their lives. You must stay alert and be aware of these changes.

Because keeping in touch and being aware of how your customers are using and adapting to new innovations will serve you well. Imagine how long your business would survive if you didn't accept credit/debit cards or bank transfers, so your customers could settle their accounts.

Have you been keeping abreast of the ever changing innovations in marketing and how to communicate with your customers? The big advert saying how wonderful you are and people are fools for not doing business with you is dead! Benefits, benefits.

I will repeat myself, benefits. Your customers are tuned into W.I.I.F.M "What's in it for me?" Are you broadcasting your messages on that wavelength? How are you using innovation to be heard on this wavelength?

The rapid pace of innovation in the last ten years alone has led to a historic shift and the re-birth of customer democracy. It is like an explosion that has had a massive splintering, growth and recognition of certain niches within each industry.

You, the business owner, has to decide how many of these splinters form the plank which creates the springboard for your business to move forward and survive. You will have to go beyond 20th Century thinking, "everyone is my customer", to find innovative ways to identify your ideal customer.

Your ideal customer will emerge from the infinite likes and dislikes within the world of niches. You will travel into niche world, identifying them and what innovations they like, believe in and expect a business to have. Because this will determine whether they become your customer or not.

This is the reality and always has been since mankind started trading with each other. Is your business innovating with things your ideal customer likes, believes and expects? Or are you a "Johnny come lately", complainer, stuck in the mud when it comes to innovation?

You may bemoan the cost of innovation, rage against the time it takes to implement and fume at the labour expended for these damn customers of yours. Because without these damn customers, your business would just be another failure.

I will leave you with a few final thoughts on innovation. How easy is it for your customers to do business with you? How quickly can they get a quote? How quickly can they place an order? How quickly can it be delivered and installed? How easy is it for them to ask questions? How long does it take your after-sales team to respond to those customer questions?

Your competitor knows, because they see innovation as an opportunity, not an inconvenience.

Hint: Never become complacent and allow the grass to grow under your feet. Keep reading and stay abreast of the trends.

Chapter 6
Appearance

"Appearances are a glimpse of the unseen".

- Aeschylus

The thesaurus says in version 4, Appearance = representation, mental representation, internal representation.

Now quickly count 1, 2, 3, 4. That's all the time it takes for your potential client to make their first impressions about your business, based on appearance. Scary? For your business to survive, thrive and avoid failure, here are some items which reflect your business appearance to others. This step done right has the potential to place you head and shoulders above your competition, in the arena of business.

The state of your bricks and mortar building. Your reception area and staff uniforms. Your website and printed materials. Your work vehicles and the design and layout of your products.

These are just a few examples but all of them make your appearance attractive to others. They affect your survival or failure in the arena of business.

In ancient Roman times people went to the arena to watch fights to the death. In modern times appearance is another arena your business must survive in to succeed.

Ever went to a brick and mortar business, stepped out of your car, took a look at the surrounding area, shook your head, got back in your car and drove off? Course you did.

Most likely the reason you turned on your heels was the state of the building and its surrounds. Probably a shabby, tired exterior, weeds and moss growing freely in the car park. The only thing missing was the obligatory tumbleweed blowing down the main drag.

Your first impression was un-kept, sloth and slovenly people and you hadn't even entered the building. You didn't even want to meet the people who had the potential to solve your problem. All because the exterior appearance screamed "we don't care". People will not give money to people who appear not to care. One of life's fundamentals.

Have you ever clicked on a website and there was so much going on, your brain overloaded and crashed? You probably have been on those sites with background colours so garish you had to wear shades. Ever browsed a website with so many ads and promos unrelated to the business you had to double check you were on the right site?

If you answered yes to all those questions, please allow me to ask you one more. Did you do any business with the company or person concerned? Or did the appearance of the site put you off taking out your credit card?

How many times has the appearance of a reception area put you off a business? You know the ones with the mismatched, cheap and nasty furniture. On the coffee table, a copy of Newsweek from the 70s, with a picture of Nixon on the cover. Dirty cups lying around. The receptionist having a wonderfully animated personal conversation whilst oblivious to your existence. Can you remember your first impression?

Like me, I imagine you have received a forest of printed materials over the years. Companies shouting their virtues and offers. After a quick glance you file them in that ever available folder....... B.U.C.K.E.T. A majority of the time the spelling and grammar was so bad you just had to stop and file. We have all done it.

Often not mentioned, except when re-telling horror stories, is the impression staff uniforms and work vehicles make on you. The cleanliness of both says a lot about a business and whether the owners care or not.

Any one of these things on their own may not be enough to put your business to step over the line and on the road to failure. Put them all together though and ask what message is your appearance saying to people with money in their pockets and a burning desire to spend it. Not a very appealing one.

It does not take much effort to paint the outside of your establishment. Less to power wash it once a year. A little bit of time and care, your car park could be inviting.

Go back, look at your website from a customer's point of view, not your rose-tinted glasses. How clean is your site? How easy is it for people to navigate? Is all the information relevant? Is the background colour easy on the eye? Is the promotion on offer relevant or confusing?

All these seemingly minor things join together to create the appearance of how your business is perceived by your current and potential customers.

Would you enjoy spending fifteen to twenty minutes in your reception area waiting for an appointment? Do you proof-read your printed material. Most often this is the first contact a person has with your business. A dirty uniform screams. "How bad are the places I can't see?" Make a deal with a local carwash for your vehicles. Be proud to hear people say "XYZ have the cleanest vehicles on the road".

Some business owners will be screaming at me right now "We have the best product/service, so why should I concern myself with all these minor things?" Probably true. The outward appearance of your business is the mirror which allows your customer form their own mental representation of your business. One that you have no control over.

One which will decide your fate. They can give you the thumbs up or the thumbs down in the arena of business.

Which will it be, thumbs up, thumbs down. Your decision!

Hint: Take pride, not only in your personal appearance but how your business appears to others.

Chapter 7
Hubris

> *"Do not believe that you alone can be right. The man who thinks that, the man who maintains that only he has the power to reason correctly the gift to speak, the soul – A man like that, when you know him turns out empty".*
>
> *- Sophocles, Antigone*

Now we have reached the final step you must overcome to avoid business failure ……..Hubris. The Chamber's dictionary describes Hubris thus – "Insolence, over-confidence, arrogance, such as leads to disaster or ruin".

Possibly this is the saddest reason of all as it appears to be self-inflicted. The ego takes over, good sense and reason are pushed aside. Anyone remember the story "The Emperor's New Clothes"?

All to often we have seen individuals and companies reach great heights of fame and fortune. They appeared to be everywhere.

Suddenly they were gone, all in the blink of an eye.

Enron, anyone?! Today they are footnotes in the annals of business. Remembered mostly for the arrogance and overconfidence that ultimately lead to their downfall.

In reality you don't have to go too far outside your local area, county, state or country to see hubris at work. Local guy makes good in one business, ego starts taking over, the leeches keep blowing hot air to keep it inflated. Next thing you know, it's all gone. They over-extended, invested in an area outside their expertise and the gods of hubris spoke and the play ended. No second act, no re-run, just an empty bank account and a busted ego.

Then you have the people and companies who become so good and so successful in their niche they believe no-one can touch them. They believe they are right. Only they have the knowledge to tell the world how things are right now, what the future holds for their industry.

This is probably the most insidious form of hubris to affect man and company. Because while they are in their ivory tower, looking down at the customer ants, living the gilded life, they take their eye off the ball.

Subtle changes start happening within their industry. Customers are searching for different, more efficient products or services. Little start-up termites have begun to nibble away at the foundations of their success.

The entrepreneurial termites start gaining market share. Nibbling away, gaining a percentage point here, a percentage point there. The business afflicted with hubris takes no notice and if they do, dismisses them as nothing but annoying termites.

Suddenly a couple of years have passed, the entrepreneurial termites have acquired a 20% market share. You call in your expert team of pest controllers, alas it's too late. The damage is too big for them to be effective. The business filled with hubris has become bloated. Attempts to strike back in vain. They have lost their nimbleness and ability to turn on a dime. Welcome to the dinosaur age.

How can this happen? It happens every day, in every town and city across the globe. No-one is immune. To avoid this happening to you, learn to control your ego. Stay flexible, stay nimble and never stop learning. Take the word "expert" out of your vocabulary. Replace it with "student". Remember, no matter how good or successful you appear to be, someone, somewhere across the globe, believes they can do it better.

Your ability to accept that the only constant in life is change, will be the mind-set that keeps your business alive and kicking. To believe that no-one could or can disrupt your dominance, is only accelerating the speed of the hubris gods to your doorstep. Compare the dominance of PCs fifteen year ago to their market share today.

Be like water, keep moving. It moves over, under, around or straight through. No obstacle can hold it back. Hubris loves inaction. It loves the ego. To stop your business failing, keep asking questions. What are you doing today that is going to give you the edge tomorrow?

You may not believe that disruptive start-ups exist. Proclaiming your greatness is all that's required to stay on top. Sorry to burst your bubble, they do exist. Open your eyes. Without them we would still be wearing the skins of animals and clubbing each other over the head to win disputes. No matter what business you are in, someone, somewhere, believes they can do a better job, provide a better product or give greater service.

It is the way of the world.

If you have reached a level of success, you deserve to be congratulated. You struggled, fought, overcame obstacles, and kept moving. You got there. Well done. Don't stand still.

Hubris is a fickle mistress.

Hint: Stay Humble
Stay Alert
Stay Real
Stay Successful

Recap

How to avoid business failure. Here is a quick look through the seven steps you need to avoid, at all cost.

1.   No System.
Flying by the seat of your pants may seem like fun but, like continuous partying, it will catch up with you. One day you will turn around and your business won't be there.

2.   R.U.B.S.
Rude, uninterested and bored staff are like military drones. You won't know they have attacked you until your business has blown up and all that's left is the debris of unpaid bills. Stay vigilant with your hiring policy.

3.   Bleed it Dry
Every living thing needs an energy source to keep it alive. Cash flow is the oxygen of your business. Don't starve it by taking, taking and putting nothing back in return.

4.   Price Loyalty
This is one hell of a slippery road to negotiate. Be prepared for the long haul. Make sure you have deep pockets. Customer loyalty is the holy grail of

business. Don't be fooled by the shiny black bauble called "price loyalty".

5.   No Innovation

If you believe that things are going to stay the same forever, maybe business is not for you. The only constant in life is change and that someone, somewhere, believes they can create a better product or service than you currently provide.

6.   Appearance

4 seconds is all the time it takes for someone to make their first impression of you and your business. Could your business survive the four second test?

7.   Hubris

Never believe your own hype. Don't surround yourself with "yes" people. Learn to control the ego. It's needed to get you started but don't let it take control and allow its first cousin, over-confidence, to join the party.

About the Author

Colin Myles has over thirty years' experience in the hospitality, transport, and manufacturing industries, dealing on a daily basis with customers and vendors alike.

Colin previously founded, with three other associates, a business referral group. He is an Author and Listener who continues to blog on the topics of business, finance and self-development.

In December 2013 his blog "Grow and Succeed" was recognised as one of the ten best blogs for entrepreneurs.

He currently lives on the wild, wet and windy Western coastline of Ireland.
His other books,

5 Keys To Doing Business With The Right People

67 Uplifting Quotes To Inspire You On Your Journey

Dedication

This book is dedicated to all of you who have taken the plunge and started your business. May you be successful.

Special thanks to my father Jim.

Many thanks to all my family, friends and associates.

A very special thank you is reserved for you for purchasing this book.

To find out more of contact Colin, go to http://www.colinmyles.net/about

36161260R00027